MOSES MAY HAVE BEEN AN APACHE!

AND OTHER Actual Facts!

BY
CULLY ABRELL & JOHN THOMPSON

THE MAIN STREET PRESS · PITTSTOWN, NEW JERSEY

PUBLISHED BY
THE MAIN STREET PRESS
WILLIAM CASE HOUSE
PITTSTOWN, NEW JERSEY   08867

PUBLISHED SIMULTANEOUSLY IN CANADA BY
McGRAW-HILL RYERSON LTD.
330 PROGRESS AVENUE
SCARBOROUGH, ONTARIO M1P 2Z5

ACKNOWLEDGMENTS

THE AUTHORS WISH TO THANK THE STATUE OF LIBERTY—ELLIS ISLAND FOUNDATION, INC.; THE OFFICE OF SUPERINTENDENT OF SCHOOLS, MATO GROSSO, FEDERATED REPUBLIC OF BRAZIL; SEA WORLD, FOR THE PORPOISE SPECIMEN; THE ENTIRE KATMANDU PORT AUTHORITY AND THEIR SPOUSES; AND IN PARTICULAR, FORMER SECRETARY OF DEFENSE ROBERT S. McNAMARA*, WITHOUT WHOSE CONTRIBUTIONS THIS WORK WOULD HAVE BEEN SHORTER.

- - - - -

*PERSONAL TO MR. McNAMARA: I HAVE A QUESTION ABOUT THE BRAKES ON MY MERCURY. CALL ME. —JT

INTRODUCTION

T WAS THEODORE ROOSEVELT WHO SAID, "AN OPEN MIND IS ONE THING; LETTING GEESE RUN AROUND IN THERE IS QUITE ANOTHER." PRESIDENT ROOSEVELT[1] KNEW THAT AS WE GROW OLDER, OUR BRAIN CELLS POP AND EXPLODE. EACH THOUGHT HOLDS A ONE-WAY TICKET TO NEUROLOGICAL PALOOKAVILLE. FACTS [WHAT WE KNOW] "PASS AWAY." OUR BRAINS PIDDLE OUT. IN DUE COURSE, EACH OF US MUST COME TO APPRECIATE THE ENORMOUS GRAVITY OF MR. ROOSEVELT'S COLORFUL DICTUM.[2]

OF COURSE, THIS IS MOSTLY METAPHORICAL. WE NOW KNOW THAT FACTS [WHAT WE KNOW] CAN BE REPLACED, IN A PROCESS NO MORE COMPLICATED THAN (AND REMARKABLY SIMILAR TO) POURING STEWED TOMATOES THROUGH A TRUMPET.[3]

IT IS TO THIS END THAT THIS WORK HAS BEEN PREPARED, AND TO THE MIGHTY WARRIOR/PEACEMAKER PRESIDENT HIMSELF[4] THAT IT IS RESPECTFULLY DEDICATED.

[1] DO NOT CONFUSE WITH PRESIDENT ROOSEVELT.
[2] ABOUT THE GEESE.
[3] SEE P. 29
[4] PRESIDENT ROOSEVELT.

ABRELL'S AND THOMPSON'S
Actual Facts!

THE FOOD SPILLED FROM TACOS IN A SINGLE AFTERNOON WOULD COMPLETELY FILL THE SHOES OF EVERYONE IN NORWAY!

THE LOST AND FOUND COLUMN OF THE DES PLAINES BUGLE HAS CARRIED THE SAME AD FOR A 4-WAY LUG WRENCH EVERY DAY FOR SOME 63 YEARS.

Lost/Found

FOUND: 4-way lug wrench. Please write Box 219

Abrell's and Thompson's Actual Facts!

VATICAN OFFICIALS ARE STILL AT A LOSS TO EXPLAIN HOW THE FAMED SHROUD OF TURIN COULD HAVE BEEN SENT TO A ONE-HOUR MARTINIZING.

FRIGHTENINGLY, AT ANY GIVEN MOMENT, AN HOUR HAS JUST PASSED.

Abrell's and Thompson's

Actual Facts!

HUMAN TEETH MAY BE SENSITIVE TO COLOR.

A MAJOR NAVAL BATTLE WAS OCCASIONED WHEN ALLIED COMMANDERS MISINTERPRETED THE REMAINS OF A CENTIPEDE ROLLED UP IN A RELIEF MAP OF THE PACIFIC THEATRE.

ABRELL'S AND THOMPSON'S
Actual Facts!

Leptinotarsa bonsai

IN ORDER TO PRESERVE THE SPECIES, SOUTHEBY'S KAMIKAZE BEETLE MUST BE KEPT FROM FLYING UNTIL AFTER IT MATES.

RADIOTELESCOPES NEAR SQUID LAKE, NEW MEXICO, HAVE DETECTED A SORT OF PECKING SOUND FROM INSIDE THE PLANET JUPITER.

ABRELL'S AND J THOMPSON'S
Actual Facts!
THE REMARKABLE SKELOSAUR WAS SO PRIMITIVE IT ACTUALLY HAD NO SKIN.
THERE HAS NEVER BEEN A MAJOR WORLD LEADER NAMED "FLOYD."

ABRELL'S AND THOMPSON'S
Actual Facts!

~OWING TO A CONGENITAL DEFECT, ONE-HALF OF HITLER'S MUSTACHE HAD TO BE PAINTED ON WITH SHOE POLISH.

•Nor•dic (nôr·d ədj. A.

THE WORD "NORDIC" ORIGINALLY DIDN'T MEAN ANYTHING.

C Abrell's and J Thompson's
Actual Facts!

BY THE TIME THE UNIVERSE
EXPLODES, "I LOVE LUCY"
WILL HAVE BEEN IN
SYNDICATION OVER
SIXTEEN BILLION
YEARS.

A TELEVISION
MACHINE OF
THE FUTURE.

THE WORST THING YOUR SHOES
CAN SMELL LIKE IS OTTERS.

ABRELL'S AND THOMPSON'S
Actual Facts!

QUEEN ELIZABETH HAS A COLLECTION OF UNUSUAL BANANAS, SOME DATING BACK TO THE 14th CENTURY.

au'to·mo·bil·ist, n. (ô'tō·mo·bēl ĭst.

ODDLY, THE OLDEST WORD IN THE ENGLISH LANGUAGE IS "AUTOMOBILIST," WHICH ORIGINALLY MEANT, "SOMEONE WHO GOES OFF BY HIMSELF."

Abrell's and Thompson's Actual Facts!

THE ROSETTA STONE WAS FOUND IN 1412, 1581, 1586, AND 1617, BUT THEY KEPT THROWING IT BACK.

MANY SCIENTISTS NOW BELIEVE THAT GRANULATED SUGAR IS ALIVE AND CAN FEEL PAIN.

OUCH.

CABRELL'S AND
J THOMPSON'S

Actual Facts!

WHEREAS THOUSANDS
OF POPULAR SONGS
CONCERN THEMSELVES
WITH LOVE AND
ROMANCE,
ONLY TWO
HAVE BEEN
WRITTEN
ABOUT
SALAD
DRESSING.

THE WORST ICE CREAM
FLAVOR IS PROBABLY
"SQUIRREL."

ABRELL'S AND THOMPSON'S
Actual Facts!

VICTOR HUGO WROTE LES MISÉRABLES OUT OF HIS DESPONDENCY OVER A MISPLACED PICKLE FORK.

MANY STATE SANITATION CODES EXPRESSLY FORBID THE RETURN OF A USED ACCORDION.

Abrell's and Thompson's Actual Facts!

JUST AS BLAKE CALLED OUR EYES "THE WINDOWS OF THE SOUL," HE REFERRED TO OUR EARS AS "THE VENTILATOR SHAFTS OF THE LIVER."

straw (strô) *n.* Th...

THE WORD "STRAW" IS ORIGINALLY FROM A LATIN WORD MEANING "BETTY."

Actual Facts!

A la recherche du temps perdu. Proust

Ma soeur, la belette Proust

MARCEL PROUST'S MONUMENTAL REMEMBRANCE OF THINGS PAST WAS FOLLOWED BY THE LESS SUCCESSFUL COMPANION VOLUME, MY SISTER WAS A WEASEL.

A GENTLEMAN IN LOTHAR, TEXAS, HAS ROPED OFF AN ADJUSTABLE DRESS FORM IN HIS ATTIC, CLAIMING IT TO BE AN INDEPENDENT REPUBLIC.

Abrell's and Thompson's

Actual Facts!

IN A STRANGE TURN OF EVENTS, SANDOW, WORLD'S TALLEST GEEK, ACTUALLY RAN AWAY FROM A CARNIVAL SIDE-SHOW TO BECOME A CONCERT PIANIST.

THE WORLD'S TALLEST GEEK, IN CONCERT.

EARLY MATHEMATICAL OPERATIONS WERE OFTEN MISLEADING BE-CAUSE MANY NUMBERS WERE NOT IN THEIR PRESENT SEQUENCE.

$1 2 3 9 7 4 8\frac{1}{2}$ ETC.

Abrell's and J Thompson's Actual Facts!

BEFORE IT WAS EDITED, THE COMMUNIST MANIFESTO CONTAINED REPEATED REFERENCES TO THE DEWEY DECIMAL SYSTEM.

BUT FOR ITS UNFORTUNATE NAME, THE STATE BIRD OF NEW MEXICO MIGHT BE THE VALIANT AND BEAUTIFUL GREENISH FLEM.

Abrell's and J Thompson's Actual Facts!

IN SOME PARTS OF THE COUNTRY THE DELICATE "FAIR MAIDEN'S TONGUE" IS KNOWN AS "PURPLE BULGARIAN STINKWORT."

THERE IS NO TRUTH TO THE RUMOR THAT CALVIN COOLIDGE WAS RAISED BY HAMSTERS.

ABRELL'S AND THOMPSON'S
Actual Facts!

ODDLY ENOUGH, THE RENAISSANCE GREW OUT OF LITIGATION OVER THE ATTEMPTED PURCHASE OF A CHICKEN.

THE LIBRETTO OF THE FIRST BALLET WAS MISPLACED ON OPENING NIGHT, THUS ESTABLISHING A SHOW-BIZ TRADITION.

CABRELL'S AND J THOMPSON'S Actual Facts!

ON A SMALLER SCALE BUT MORE INTERESTING HISTORICALLY THAN JACKSON HOLE, WYOMING, IS TINY OUT-OF-THE-WAY LAVERN'S HOLE, ALBERTA, WHERE FRANK LAVERN HOLED UP FOR TWENTY YEARS AFTER DREAMING HE ROBBED A BANK.

Admit One. LAVERN'S HOLE. № 000036

ABRAHAM LINCOLN INTENDED THE GETTYSBURG ADDRESS TO BE A SONG! —

THE SCORE FOR FOURSCORE

ABRELL'S AND THOMPSON'S
Actual Facts!

STRANGELY, THE COMMON SAUSAGE CADDY DID NOT ENJOY ITS' PRESENT POPULARITY UNTIL THE LATE 1950'S.

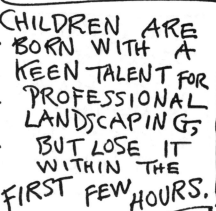

CHILDREN ARE BORN WITH A KEEN TALENT FOR PROFESSIONAL LANDSCAPING, BUT LOSE IT WITHIN THE FIRST FEW HOURS.

ABRELL'S AND J THOMPSON'S

Actual Facts!

THE WORLD'S SMALLEST BOULDER FITS EASILY INSIDE AN ORDINARY HAT BOX.

THE ORDINARY SOCK DID NOT CATCH ON UNTIL THE SECOND ONE WAS INVENTED SOME 800 YEARS LATER.

ca.950

A.D. 1748

Abrell's and Thompson's Actual Facts!

POTATOES WERE NOT WIDELY ACCEPTED UNTIL THE DEVELOPMENT OF TODAY'S BONELESS VARIETIES!

THERE IS A CEMETERY IN GLASGOW EXCLUSIVELY FOR BAGPIPES!

Cabrell's and J Thompson's
Actual Facts!

THE FUNNEL WAS INVENTED WHEN A MAN TRIED TO POUR STEWED TOMATOES THROUGH A TRUMPET.

A WOMAN IN BELOIT, WISCONSIN ENJOYS LISTENING TO CHEESE.

ABRELL'S AND J THOMPSON'S

Actual Facts!

RECENTLY DISCOVERED LETTERS TO HIS MOTHER REVEAL THAT CHAS. DARWIN DESPERATELY LONGED FOR MORE BODY HAIR.

THE WORST TRUE STORY EVER PUBLISHED WAS "THE DAY I MET ANTOINE SMEKKERT" BY BONITA WHIZZER.

Actual Facts!

ABRELL'S AND J THOMPSON'S

BECAUSE SO MANY HAVE ABUSED THE PRIVILEGE, IT MAY SOON BE ILLEGAL TO SEND COTTAGE CHEESE THROUGH THE MAIL.

UNSCRUPULOUS FILM PRODUCERS MADE "HAMMURABI, WRATH OF BABYLON" BY ADDING AN EXPLANATORY PROLOGUE TO "THE PREVIOUSLY RELEASED "THE DREAMS OF MRS. FRANKLIN PIERCE."

Abrell's and Thompson's
Actual Facts!

BERT'S ANTSUCKER, WHEN AROUSED, EMITS THE DISTINCT ODOR OF CREAMED SPINACH, ACCORDING TO MURRAY WERTNEW.

IF ALL THE TONGUES SCALDED BY CHICKEN SOUP IN A SINGLE WEEK WERE LAID END-TO-END, THEY WOULD STRETCH FROM MONTPELIER, VERMONT, ALMOST TO THE OUTSKIRTS OF HIBBING, MINNESOTA.

~ABRELL'S AND J THOMPSON'S
Actual Facts!

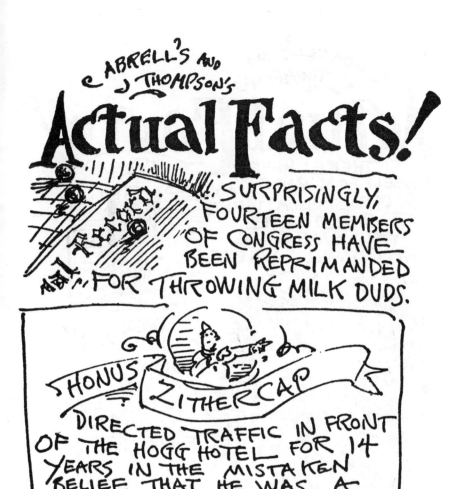

SURPRISINGLY, FOURTEEN MEMBERS OF CONGRESS HAVE BEEN REPRIMANDED FOR THROWING MILK DUDS.

BONUS! ZITHERCAP

DIRECTED TRAFFIC IN FRONT OF THE HOGG HOTEL FOR 14 YEARS IN THE MISTAKEN BELIEF THAT HE WAS A MEMBER OF THE GRETNA, NEBRASKA POLICE DEPARTMENT.

Abrell's and J Thompson's
Actual Facts!

THERE HAVE BEEN FOUR PARTIALLY SUCCESSFUL ATTEMPTS TO RELOCATE YELLOWSTONE NATIONAL PARK.

— OLD FAITHFUL.

IN ORDER TO CUT COURT COSTS, QUEEN ELIZABETH I RELUCTANTLY EXPUNGED FOUR LETTERS FROM THE ENGLISH ALPHABET.

Actual Facts!

ANCIENT CLOTH FRAGMENTS SHOW THAT "STRIPES" WERE SOMEWHAT SHORTER THAN THEY ARE TODAY.

THE WORST HABIT A PARAKEET CAN DEVELOP IS SPITTING.

ABRELL'S AND THOMPSON'S
Actual Facts!

SAMUEL "F.B." MORSE DEVISED HIS FAMOUS "CODE" IN ORDER TO COMMUNICATE WITH THE SPIRIT OF HIS DEAD WOODPECKER, "CLIFFORD."

OVER A SIX-YEAR PERIOD CROWN PRINCE LUDWIG SECRETLY MAILED PRESIDENT WOODROW WILSON FOUR HUNDRED PAIRS OF BALLET SLIPPERS.

Abrell's and Thompson's

Actual Facts!

IT IS SOBERING TO REALIZE THAT ALMOST EVERYTHING IS ONE DIRECTION OR ANOTHER FROM KANSAS CITY.

KANSAS

A FIFTEENTH CENTURY MUSEUM OF THE FOOLISH IN ZURICH IS NOW TAKEN SERIOUSLY.

Abrell's and Thompson's
Actual Facts!

ALTHOUGH MOST GEOLOGICAL FEATURES "RECYCLE," IT IS GENERALLY AGREED THAT THERE ARE STILL TRACES OF THE ORIGINAL WIND.

EARTH'S CORE

TEXAS.

MOST STATES FIT SO CLOSELY TOGETHER THAT ALMOST NO SPACE IS WASTED.

ABRELL'S AND J THOMPSON'S

Actual Facts!

LIKE THE ATOM, THE FLYSWATTER CAN BE A FORCE FOR GREAT GOOD OR GREAT EVIL.

ALBERT EINSTEIN AND HIS TWIN BROTHER BOTH INSISTED THEY BE PHOTOGRAPHED SEPARATELY!

ABRELL'S AND THOMPSON'S Actual Facts!

NEW EVIDENCE SUGGESTS THAT NORMAL BODY TEMPERATURE IS 89.4° AND THAT MANKIND IS RUNNING A TEMPERATURE.

THE WORST NOVEL EVER WRITTEN WAS SMEKKERT'S 1934 EFFORT, "A POTATO FOR BEVERLY."

Abrell's and Thompson's Actual Facts!

LIGHTNING IS ATTRACTED MORE TO CHINESE CABBAGE THAN TO ANY OTHER COMMON VEGETABLE CROP.

LESTER SMELT OF TREEBLE, NEW HAMPSHIRE, HAS BUILT A WORKING PENCIL SHARPENER AS BIG AS A CAR.

Abrell's and J. Thompson's Actual Facts!

AMBROSE WIMPLE OF DUCK NOSTRIL, TENNESSEE, HAS INADVERTENTLY EATEN OVER 50 PAIRS OF SUSPENDERS.

THE SHORTEST-LIVED DANCE CRAZE WAS "THE EXPECTORATE."

ABRELL'S AND THOMPSON'S
Actual Facts!

THE SINGLE MOST DESCRIPTIVE
PHRASE EVER TO APPEAR IN
AN AMERICAN NOVEL WAS THE
TERSE SIMILE, "QUIET AS ED."

quiet as Ed.

KINDLY ♡ ESTHER
THREADWICKE HAS
MADE A COOKIE
FOR EVERYONE
IN NOVA SCOTIA.

Abrell's and J. Thompson's
Actual Facts!

HUBBARD J. FARDHOOPLE CONTENDS THAT, FOR THE PAST 30 YEARS, HE HAS REPAIRED AN INTERNATIONAL HARVESTER WITH PARTS GROWN IN HIS GARDEN.

A FULL SET OF DRILL BITS COMPRISED OF EVERY POSSIBLE SIZE WOULD COMPLETELY FILL THE KNOWN UNIVERSE!

ABRELL'S AND J THOMPSON'S
Actual Facts!

ONE OF THE LEAST APPRECIATED FIGURES IN AMERICAN HISTORY WAS PRESIDENT LELAND PIATT.

HALF WAY AROUND THE WORLD IS ACTUALLY FARTHER AWAY THAN ALL THE WAY AROUND!

ABRELL'S AND J THOMPSON'S
Actual Facts!

THE ANCIENT MAYAS WERE, IN ALL BUT ONE RESPECT, COMPLETELY PREPARED TO RECEIVE COMMERCIAL RADIO BROADCASTS.

A RECENT SHIPMENT OF GRAPEFRUIT FROM MEXICO CONTAINED AN ENTIRE FORK-LIFT TRUCK.

ABRELL'S AND THOMPSON'S
Actual Facts!

PRESENT-DAY
LAND ASSESSMENTS
ARE AN OUT-
GROWTH OF
THE OLD SAXON
WORM TAX.

IN COSMIC TERMS
THE REAL UNIVERSE
MAY BE ABOUT
THE SIZE OF A
SMALL PEACH.

¿ABRELL'S AND ♪ THOMPSON'S

Actual Facts!

IRONICALLY, HERNANDO SUFFOCATED IN A MIGRATION.

FIELD MARSHAL CIVET LEMMING

TRADITION HOLDS THAT SOCCER WAS BORN WHEN A DISTRAUGHT PEASANT WOMAN DELIBERATELY KICKED A SPHERE OF RANCID GOAT CHEESE INTO A YARD FULL OF MONKS.

C. ABRELL'S AND J THOMPSON'S
Actual Facts!

VISITORS TO THE INFAMOUS PILTDOWN WORLD'S FAIR WERE GREETED BY A STATUE CALLED "THE SPIRIT OF MEAT".

TO STATUE

FIELD MARSHAL HERNANDO CIVET, 64, 7B, distinguished veteran of the last war, perished

OBITUARIES OF THE 19TH CENTURY TRADITIONALLY INCLUDED THE DECEASED'S SHOE SIZE.

ABRELL'S AND THOMPSON'S Actual Facts!

MELODIA COMPOST SUFFERED WITH INDEFATIGABLE SNEEZING FITS FOR 102 YEARS WHEN, REMARKABLY, SHE WAS CURED, AND FELL ASLEEP EXHAUSTED, AND DIED.

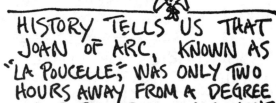

HISTORY TELLS US THAT JOAN OF ARC, KNOWN AS "LA POUCELLE", WAS ONLY TWO HOURS AWAY FROM A DEGREE IN FORESTRY MANAGEMENT.

Abrell's and Thompson's
Actual Facts!

THE LATE ALFRED NORTH WHITEHEAD CLAIMED TO HAVE SLICED A TOMATO SO THAT IT WAS WORTH OVER $10,000.

THE INABILITY OF SNAKES TO COUNT IS NOTHING MORE THAN AN UNWILLINGNESS ON THEIR PART TO APPRECIATE THE CARDINAL NUMBER SYSTEM.

ABRELL'S AND J THOMPSON'S
Actual Facts!

TWO OF THE WORLD'S LARGEST STAMP COLLECTIONS ARE OWNED BY DOGS, BUT THEY ARE WORTHLESS BECAUSE THEY HAVE BEEN LICKED AND BURIED.

GRAVEROBBING IS LITTLE MORE THAN CONTEMPORARY ARCHAEOLOGY.

cABRELL'S AND J THOMPSON'S
Actual Facts!

NOW GENERALLY OMIT-
TED FROM THE OPENING
CEREMONIES OF THE
HOUSE OF LORDS IS THE
"PERCIVAL PARAGRAPH,"
CONCERNING
ROBE ODOR.

THE PERSONAL HERO
OF ZORRO, THE
GENTLEMAN AVENGER,
WAS ANGUS MAC FINNART,
A SHEET METAL WORKER
FROM WEE BANKIE.

Abrell's and Thompson's Actual Facts!

THE OLDER YOU GET, THE LESS FUNNY SOME THINGS MAY SEEM.

SOMETIMES THE "TRUTH" AND THE "OUTRAGEOUS" ARE DIFFICULT TO DISTINGUISH.

Abrell's and J Thompson's Actual Facts!

EVERY DAY FOR THE LAST 31 YEARS SOMEONE HAS LEFT A SINGLE ROLLER SKATE AT THE TOMB OF KING VICTOR EMMANUEL II.

THE EPONYMOUS ARDMORE W. JEEPERS WAS THE FIRST PERSON EVER TO STICK HIS FORK INTO A "LIVE" TOASTER.

Abrell's and Thompson's Actual Facts!

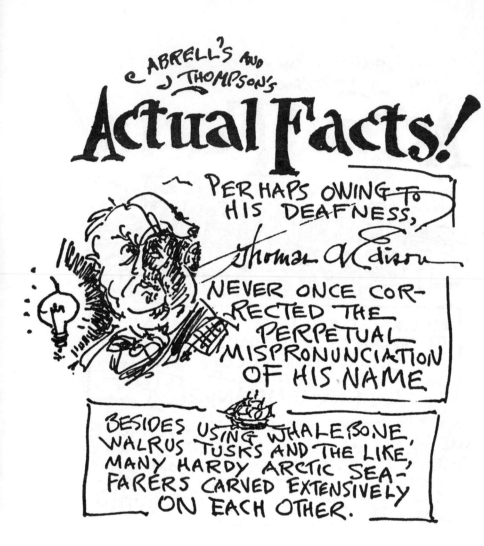

Perhaps owing to his deafness, Thomas A. Edison never once corrected the perpetual mispronunciation of his name.

Besides using whalebone, walrus tusks and the like, many hardy Arctic sea-farers carved extensively on each other.

Abrell's and Thompson's Actual Facts!

A PROTRACTED METAPHOR IN A REFRIGERATOR SERVICE MANUAL INCLUDED THE NAMES AND ADDRESSES OF EVERYONE IN PORT NORRIS, N.J.

PHILADELPHIA

NEW JERSEY

THE ATLANTIC

FEDERAL INSPECTORS WERE STARTLED TO DISCOVER A MINT 1935 STUDEBAKER "BROUGHAM" PRESERVED IN A VAT OF VEGETABLE SHORTENING.

ABRELL'S AND THOMPSON'S
Actual Facts!

BOB'S SOAPATORIUM: STATISTICALLY, THE ULTIMATE HIGH-RISK ENTERPRISE IS THE FIELD OF SOAP RENTAL.

ZUKKER BLITZCAN HAS DISCOVERED A NEW COLOR BETWEEN PUCE AND VERMILLION WHICH HE CALLS "VERMILLIPUCE!"

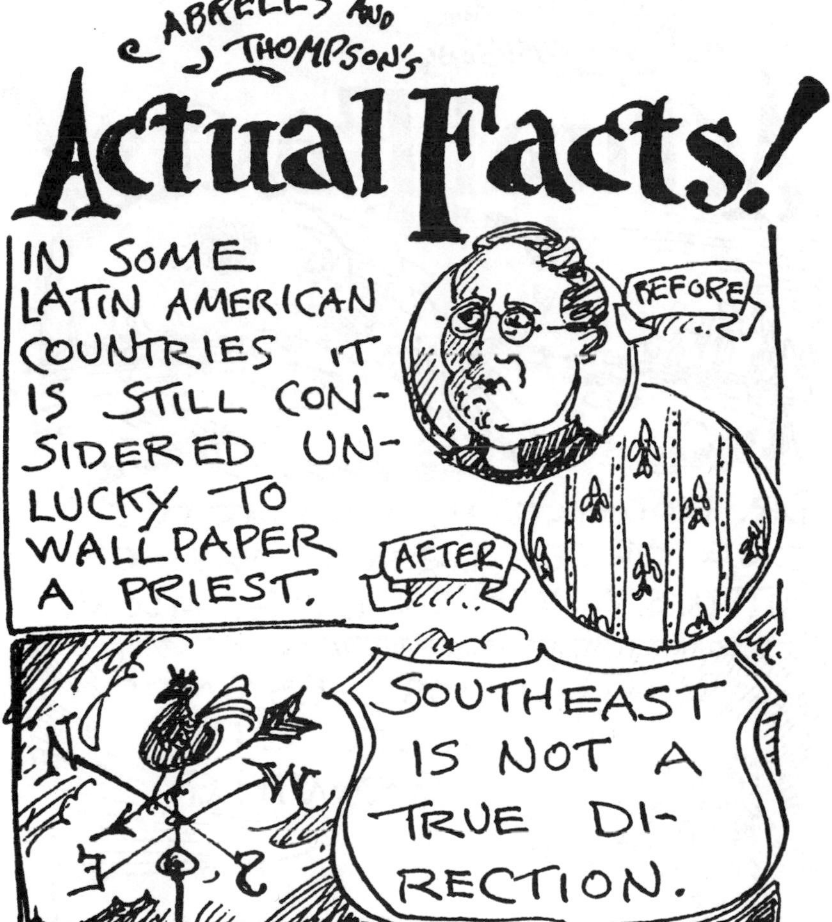

ABRELL'S AND THOMPSON'S
Actual Facts!
IN SOME LATIN AMERICAN COUNTRIES IT IS STILL CONSIDERED UNLUCKY TO WALLPAPER A PRIEST.
BEFORE
AFTER
SOUTHEAST IS NOT A TRUE DIRECTION.

Actual Facts!

CABRELL'S AND J THOMPSON'S

DR. ROBERT H. GODDARD'S ONE TRUE DREAM WAS OF PUTTING A WIENER ON THE MOON.

'MOST ESKIMOS NEVER STOP GROWING,

Abrell's and Thompson's Actual Facts!

— THE MAN WHO PENNED THE MUSICAL PHRASE "TIDDLEY-POM" GREW RICH AND FAMOUS, WHILE THE AUTHOR OF "TRA LA, TRA LA" DIED IN SHAME AND PENURY. —

SHAMEFULLY, IT IS PERFECTLY LEGAL TO THROW SPOONS AT THE STATUE OF LIBERTY.

ABRELL'S AND J THOMPSON'S

Actual Facts!

"HAIL TO THE CHIEF" COMES FROM THE OLD ENGLISH SEA CHANTY "HEY NONNY NONNY, KNOCK THE WEEVILS OFF YOUR BISCUIT."

ORIGINALLY, THE HOUR WAS AN ARBITRARY PERIOD OF TIME.

ABRELL'S AND THOMPSON'S
Actual Facts!
SURPRISINGLY FEW PEOPLE EVER REMEMBER TO CHANGE THE FLUID IN THEIR RADIOS
MICHELANGELO'S "DAVID" CONTAINS ENOUGH MARBLE TO MAKE 62,000 PAPERWEIGHTS.

Abrell's and J Thompson's Actual Facts!

EXCAVATIONS AROUND THE HISTORIC ARCH OF HADRIAN HAVE UNEARTHED A DISTURBING NUMBER OF PECULIAR VACUUM CLEANER ATTACHMENTS.

THE WORLD'S LEAST SUCCESSFUL GAME SHOW WAS CALLED **BOWLING FOR SKUNK CABBAGE**

Actual Facts!

ABRELL'S AND THOMPSON'S

A CAPRICE OF MOTHER NATURE HAS GRADUALLY TURNED THE HUMAN TONGUE INSIDE OUT.

BEFORE ESPERANTO WAS A LANGUAGE, IT WAS A CAR.

ABRELL'S AND J THOMPSON'S

Actual Facts!

IT IS IMPORTANT TO NOTE THAT THE AVERAGE AGE OF MOST SO-CALLED 'LIVING FOSSILS' IS ONLY 19.

LEARN HYPNOTISM.

Price POSTPAID 25¢ 3 for $1.00

TURTLES SHIPPED BY MAIL
25¢
$1.00 (LIVE)

MAKE GREAT PETS. GET 'EM

THREE DAYS TO A BETTER NOSE! IMPROVE YOUR.

THE PHRASE, "A PENNY FOR YOUR THOUGHTS" HAS FILTERED DOWN TO US FROM THE OLD CELTIC EXPRESSION, "A SHEEPDOG FOR YOUR SISTER."

Abrell's and Thompson's
Actual Facts!

DESPITE HIS RE-
MARKABLE MEM-
ORY AND STUN-
NINGLY UNERR-
ING EYE FOR
DETAIL, LEONAR-
DO DA VINCI OFTEN
CALLED LOREN-
ZO DE MEDICI
"MR. STEADMAN."

A CANAL IN BAVARIA
CONNECTS TWO GREAT
BODIES OF SAND.

FÜRSTEN-
FELDBRUCK

BAV.

CABRELL'S AND J THOMPSON'S Actual Facts!

BLAND ISLANDS 5 N°

JUST IN CASE SHE GOT CAUGHT IN A TIME WARP, PIONEER AVIATRIX AMELIA EARHART ALWAYS CARRIED AN ENORMOUS BAG OF LUCKY NICKELS.

ALL FOOD CAN BE PLACED MORE OR LESS IN THE 'BROCCOLI' FAMILY.

ABRELL'S AND THOMPSON'S
Actual Facts!

THE DAILY FORMICARIAN

DOG LICKS OLD SUCKER

MISSING!

1,000'S PERISH!

YET ANOTHER ANT WAR

SOLDIER MASQUERADES AS NURSE

TODAYS DEATHS

A NEWS-PAPER PUBLISHED BY ANTS WOULD CONSIST PRIMARILY OF OBITUARIES.

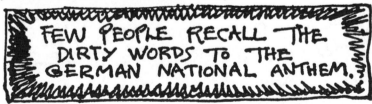

FEW PEOPLE RECALL THE DIRTY WORDS TO THE GERMAN NATIONAL ANTHEM.

ABRELL'S AND THOMPSON'S
Actual Facts!

TO CALL ANYTHING "RECTILINEAR" IN VICTORIAN ENGLAND COULD RESULT IN CRIMINAL PROSECUTION.

THE FIRST DOORKNOB WAS FAR SUPERIOR TO THOSE WE HAVE TODAY.

e ABRELL'S AND J THOMPSON'S
Actual Facts!

THERE HAS NEVER BEEN A SCIENCE FICTION NOVEL IN WHICH ALIENS ATTACKED THE UNITED KINGDOM OF GREAT BRITAIN AND NORTHERN IRELAND AND DEMANDED MONEY.

'orki (gor'kē), n. 1. / LITERALLY, "BITTER" IN RUSSIAN MAXIM GORKI IS ALSO LATIN FOR, "THE LARGEST AMOUNT OF ANYTHING YOU CAN COUGH UP.=

Abrell's and Thompson's Actual Facts!

THE LATE VLADMIR PRUNEHAUS OF TWIDDINGWADDLE-ON-ORKNEY, NORWAY, PRODUCED OVER 40 PALINDROMES USING ONLY NUMBERS!

"2121212121212121 2"——

OF THE DOMESTIC ANIMALS, SHEEP ARE GENERALLY THE LEAST APPRECIATIVE.

Abrell's and Thompson's Actual Facts!

MANY SNAKES ARE ACTUALLY QUITE SHORT, IF YOU DON'T COUNT THE TAIL.

ALWAYS A PRAC-
TICAL JOKER,
RHODESIAN STATESMAN
NG!ANG EBOUBI, JR.
ONCE GAVE MA-
HATMA GANDHI
A HOT-FOOT.

EUROPEAN VIPER.

ABRELL'S AND THOMPSON'S
Actual Facts!

FELLOPIA DORKING OF WAVERLY-ON-DAVENPORT, UNITED KINGDOM, HAS DEMONSTRATED THAT A CHICKEN'S CAPACITY TO REASON MEASURABLY IN-CREASES WHEN ITS HEAD IS REMOVED.

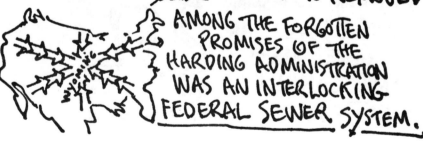

AMONG THE FORGOTTEN PROMISES OF THE HARDING ADMINISTRATION WAS AN INTERLOCKING FEDERAL SEWER SYSTEM.

ABRELL'S AND THOMPSON'S Actual Facts!

THE ONLY SCROLL TO SURVIVE THE FIRE IN THE LIBRARY AT ALEXANDRIA WAS DEVOTED TO THE THEORY OF MASCARA.

DOGS USE THEIR FACES ONLY ABOUT HALF AS MUCH AS PEOPLE DO.

Abrell's and Thompson's Actual Facts!

A PLANARIAN CAN BE TRAINED TO FORGET EVERYTHING IT KNOWS!

THE KANSAS FISH AND GAME COMMISSION REGULARLY FINES THADDEUS FEKKNER FOR PLAYING "AMAZING GRACE" ON HIS DUCK CALL.

Abrell's and Thompson's Actual Facts!

EZRA POUND WENT TO VENICE IN ORDER TO GET AWAY FROM PEOPLE AND SEWERS.

"PERHAPS THE SADDEST REMINDER OF THE PASSAGE OF TIME HAS BEEN THE LUMINOUS YO-YO."

Abrell's and Thompson's
Actual Facts!

A MODEL 🏰 OF THE HUMAN IMMUNE SYSTEM CARVED OUT OF LARD AND DONATED TO THE SMITHSONIAN HAS SINCE BEEN MOVED TO AN OUTBUILDING.

CLEVERLY CONCEALED FROM PUBLIC VIEW IN YELLOWSTONE NATIONAL PARK ARE THE OTHER HALF OF THE GEYSERS, WHICH FLUSH.

NOT A GEYSER KEEP AWAY

Abrell's and Thompson's Actual Facts!

MRS. INEZ FOON, OF BIGGARSTOAT, STEADFASTLY MAINTAINS THAT SHE COMES FROM A LONGER LINE OF ANCESTORS THAN ANYONE ELSE.

BECAUSE DENTISTS OFTEN USED PATIENTS' TEETH AS CHRISTMAS TREE ORNAMENTS, SURGEONS WERE NOT ALLOWED TO DECORATE THEIR OFFICES AT ALL.

Abrell's and Thompson's
Actual Facts!

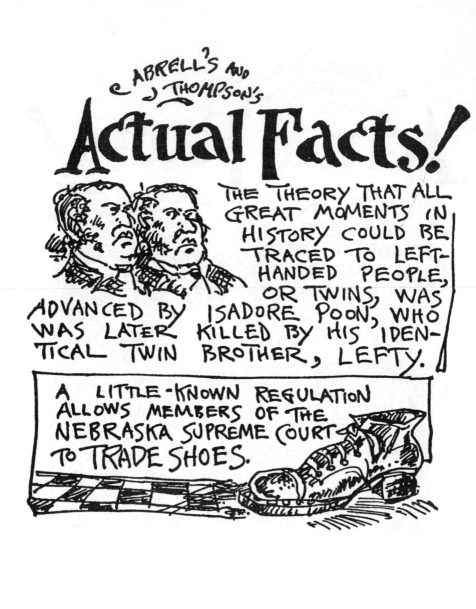

THE THEORY THAT ALL GREAT MOMENTS IN HISTORY COULD BE TRACED TO LEFT-HANDED PEOPLE, OR TWINS, WAS ADVANCED BY ISADORE POON, WHO WAS LATER KILLED BY HIS IDENTICAL TWIN BROTHER, LEFTY.

A LITTLE-KNOWN REGULATION ALLOWS MEMBERS OF THE NEBRASKA SUPREME COURT TO TRADE SHOES.

ABRELL'S AND
THOMPSON'S

Actual Facts!

IT MAY BE POSSIBLE TO SUE CANADA FOR THE ICE AGE.

DOMINION OF CANADA

BAY OF HUDSON

USA

UPON VIEWING THE PACIFIC OCEAN FOR THE FIRST TIME, VASCO NUÑEZ DE BALBOA IS REPUTED TO HAVE MUTTERED, "DAMMIT, WE'VE WALKED IN A CIRCLE."

ABRELL'S AND THOMPSON'S
Actual Facts!

A PROMINENT WASHINGTON SOCIALITE WAS FINED BY THE LIBRARY OF CONGRESS FOR DRAWING LIVER SPOTS ON PHOTOGRAPHS OF THE FIRST LADY.

NAPOLEON BONAPARTE DISMISSED FINLAND AS "A NATION OF CHIRO-PRACTORS." — Napoleon

ABRELL'S AND J THOMPSON'S
Actual Facts!

SCIENTISTS HAVE ISOLATED A NOISE MADE JUST PRIOR TO THE "BIG BANG" WHICH SOUNDS SOMETHING LIKE "OOPS."

WHILE, IT IS TRUE THAT "THERE'S NO TIME LIKE THE PRESENT," IT IS EQUALLY TRUE THAT THERE IS NO TIME LIKE LAST THURSDAY.

ABRELL'S AND J THOMPSON'S

Actual Facts!

THOUGH NOT OUR LARGEST STATE IN SQUARE MILES, WISCONSIN IS PROBABLY OUR THICKEST.

N DAK · MINN. · WISC. · S. DAK · IOWA · ILL.

AUSTRALIA WAS THE FIRST COUNTRY NOT TO REQUIRE THAT WOMEN PLAY CELLO SIDESADDLE.

Abrell's and Thompson's
Actual Facts!

ACTUARIALLY, IT NOW COSTS MORE TO INSURE A FASHION MODEL AGAINST HIP DISLOCATION THAN IT DOES A RUGBY PLAYER.

PAVLOV HAD LITTLE SUCCESS UNTIL HE REPLACED COCOANUTS WITH DOGS.

Abrell's and J Thompson's Actual Facts!

NOT ONLY DID NOSTRADAMAS FORGET ABOUT THE 1915 PANAMA-PACIFIC EXPOSITION, HE MISSPELLED "EDSEL."

ALTHOUGH IT IS HARD TO IMAGINE, THE FIRST DRUMS WERE SUPPOSED TO BE BLOWN.

Abrell's and Thompson's Actual Facts!

CABRELL'S AND J THOMPSON'S

OVER THE COURSE OF THE NEXT SEVERAL CENTURIES, THE CONSTELLATION VULPECULA WILL COME TO RESEMBLE ANNE BOLEYN.

A SWEET POTATO SHAPED LIKE MAO TSE-TUNG MADE MORE MONEY IN TWO WEEKS THAN PETER BRUEGEL THE ELDER MADE IN HIS ENTIRE LIFETIME.

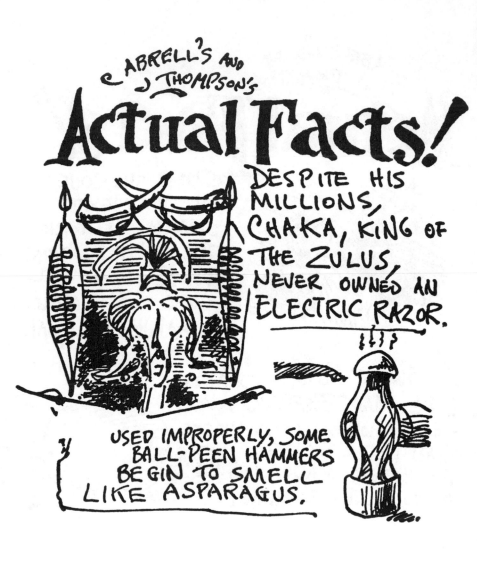

ABRELL'S AND J THOMPSON'S

Actual Facts!

DESPITE HIS MILLIONS, CHAKA, KING OF THE ZULUS, NEVER OWNED AN ELECTRIC RAZOR.

USED IMPROPERLY, SOME BALL-PEEN HAMMERS BEGIN TO SMELL LIKE ASPARAGUS.

ABRELL'S AND J THOMPSON'S
Actual Facts!

LARS OLAFSON WAS PUT TO SLEEP BY THE GOVERNMENT OF DENMARK FOR "BEING TOO HELPFUL."

"CAMEL" IS FROM THE ANCIENT ARABIC, "PENGUIN OF THE DESERT."

ABRELL'S AND THOMPSON'S
Actual Facts!

ALFRED B. NOBEL'S FAVORITE BOOK WAS "THE ROMANCE OF ALUMINUM."

THE ORIGINAL DESIGN FOR THE FLAG OF ECUADOR INCLUDED A SMALL REFRIGERATOR.

ABRELL'S AND THOMPSON'S
Actual Facts!

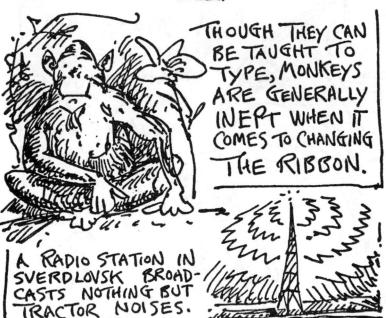

THOUGH THEY CAN BE TAUGHT TO TYPE, MONKEYS ARE GENERALLY INEPT WHEN IT COMES TO CHANGING THE RIBBON.

A RADIO STATION IN SVERDLOVSK BROAD- CASTS NOTHING BUT TRACTOR NOISES.

ABRELL'S AND
THOMPSON'S

Actual Facts!

♪ A MAN IN WHITNEY, UTAH, KNOWS OVER 6000 WAYS TO MISSPELL "SOUSA-PHONES."

THE TINY CHADWEE IS NATURE'S STRANGEST ANIMAL.

Abrell's and Thompson's Actual Facts!

— AS WITH THE ICEBERG, MUCH OF THE EARTH'S LAND-MASS LIES BENEATH THE SURFACE.

FRENCH, AS IT IS NOW SPOKEN, IS NOT A REAL LANGUAGE.

"LES CHAMPIGNONS"?

ABRELL'S AND J THOMPSON'S
Actual Facts!

THE ORIGINAL POLKA DOT HAS BEEN CAREFULLY PRESERVED IN A TEXTILE MUSEUM NEAR BRUSSELS.

THE SCHWASSMANN-WACHMANN CHAMELEON CAN BE USED AS AN ERASER.

ABRELL'S AND THOMPSON'S

Actual Facts!

BENJAMIN FRANKLIN HAD NO FACE. ALL PAINTINGS, ENGRAVINGS AND STATUARY OF THE FAMOUS STATESMAN ARE MERELY ARTISTS' CONCEPTIONS.

UNDER THE LAW, DENTISTS ARE FORBIDDEN FROM WEARING ARTIFICIAL NOSES.

ABRELL'S AND THOMPSON'S

Actual Facts!

A SPECULATIVE RECONSTRUCTION OF THE LOVELY VENUS DE MILO SHOWS HER HOLDING A PARROT.

BLAND ISLAND
.0004 NOSES

THE MONETARY SYSTEM OF THE BLAND ISLANDS IS BASED ENTIRELY ON A SET OF IRON NOSES.

ABRELL'S AND THOMPSON'S
Actual Facts!

MYSTERIOUSLY, KING TUTANKHAMEN'S PERSONAL EFFECTS INCLUDED THE KEY TO A SAFETY DEPOSIT BOX.

UNLIKE HIS PNEUMATIC TIRES, HARVEY FIRESTONE'S CHUNKY TOOTHPASTE NEVER QUITE CAUGHT ON.

HARVEY FIRESTONE'S CHUNKY TOOTHPASTE

Actual Facts!

IF PEOPLE WERE ELIMINATED FROM THE EARTH, 72¢ OUT OF EVERY DOLLAR COULD BE SAVED.

IT IS CONSIDERED ILL-MANNERED TO SERVE HORS D'OEUVRES ON A SNOWSHOE.

Abrell's and J Thompson's
Actual Facts!

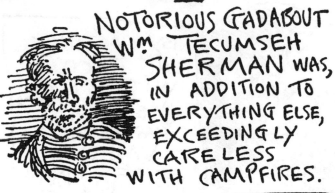

NOTORIOUS GADABOUT W.m TECUMSEH SHERMAN WAS, IN ADDITION TO EVERYTHING ELSE, EXCEEDINGLY CARELESS WITH CAMPFIRES.

THE WORLD'S WORST LOVE SONG IS ENTITLED "I'LL LOVE YOU 'TIL YOU'RE DEAD"

ABRELL'S AND THOMPSON'S
Actual Facts!

BY COATING HIS FACE WITH PLASTIC, JEELY KRUTZ HAS GROWN A VAN DYKE INSIDE HIS MOUTH

BECAUSE OF RECENT FINDINGS IN A DIG NEAR TUCSON, ARCHAEOLOGISTS NOW BELIEVE MOSES TO HAVE BEEN AN APACHE

Abrell's and Thompson's Actual Facts!

THE U.S. PATENT OFFICE REFUSED TO LICENCE THE COMMON B·B BECAUSE THEY REQUIRE TWO VIEWS!

U.S PATENT OFFICE.

Bell out of order. Come in.

LA SALLE SUCKSNYDER OF PERU, IOWA, HAS OVER 6,000 SUITCASES FILLED WITH PANCAKES.

Abrell's and Thompson's
Actual Facts!

ANANDAS "PIG LIPS" WALLABY WAS THE ONLY MAN EVER TO EAT TOAST THROUGH A HUBCAP.

POSTMASTER GENERAL JAMES A. FARLEY DESTROYED AN ENTIRE PRINTING OF STAMPS PURPORTING TO HONOR THE AMERICAN SHOEHORN.

ABRELL'S AND J THOMPSON'S

Actual Facts!

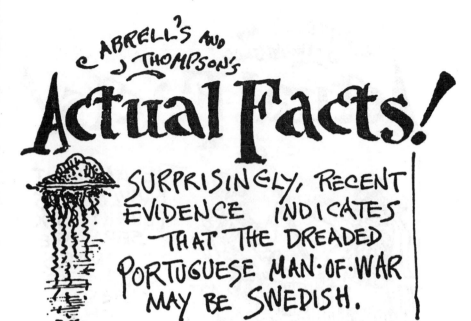

SURPRISINGLY, RECENT EVIDENCE INDICATES THAT THE DREADED PORTUGUESE MAN·OF·WAR MAY BE SWEDISH.

FROM THE STAND-POINT OF THE LAW, IT IS BETTER TO HIT A CONGRESSMAN OVER THE HEAD WITH A SKILLET THAN IT IS TO CALL HIM "A SNIVELING NEMATODE."

ABRELL'S AND THOMPSON'S
Actual Facts!

THE ANCIENT BABYLONIANS FOUGHT SIX SEPARATE WARS OVER THE POSSESSION OF A MAGIC FISH.

THE TRUCK MUFFLER WAS ACTUALLY INVENTED IN 1710, BUT MET WITH LITTLE SUCCESS.

Abrell's and Thompson's Actual Facts!

SUCCESS! | FAILURE!

ALWAYS ONE STEP AWAY FROM GREATNESS, RUFUS W. ORTFUNDLER DEVELOPED PAPER BAGS WHICH OPENED AT THE OPPOSING END AND THUS WERE DEEMED ENTIRELY USELESS!

NO ONE IS REALLY CERTAIN THERE IS A COUNTRY CALLED "RUMANIA!"

ABRELL'S AND J THOMPSON'S

Actual Facts!

IRONICALLY, A NEWT'S BACK LEGS ARE ON FRONTWARDS.

IF YOU CUT THE AUSTRALIAN BAZOORY TREE IN HALF, YOU WILL HAVE FOUR PIECES!

ABRELL'S AND THOMPSON'S
Actual Facts!
THE WORST SNACK FOOD IDEA WAS A PRODUCT CALLED "RAT LUNGS."
25¢
RAT LUNGS
GROSVENOR, UTAH HAS BEEN DESIGNATED THE "SISTER" CITY OF GROSVENOR, UTAH.
WELCOME TO GROSVENOR
WELCOME TO GROSVENOR

ABRELL'S AND THOMPSON'S
Actual Facts!

HARRISTOWN, PENNSYLVANIA WAS NAMED IN HONOR OF ITS FOUNDER, JACK LOGAN.

Bad Boot Bugle 15¢
- EXTRA -
TWO CHICKENS ALIKE!

NEWSPAPER ACCOUNTS FROM THE 1920's DESCRIBE THE BRIEF APPEARANCE OF TWO COMPLETELY IDENTICAL CHICKENS NEAR BAD BOOT, UTAH, A SUBURB OF GROSVENOR.

ABRELL'S AND J THOMPSON'S

Actual Facts!

EXCEPT FOR THE NOTORIOUS TRAGEDIES BY GASTON PILLOWDEW, FEW PLAYS HAVE REVOLVED AROUND THE CENTRAL THEME OF CAT-NEUTERING.

TWO IDENTICAL SNOW FLAKES FELL OVER GROSVENOR, UTAH, IN 1927.

ABRELL'S AND THOMPSON'S

Actual Facts!

PRIOR TO STRIKING, THE DREADED RUFOUS BUSHMASTER WILL HONK.

THOUGH REMEMBERED FOR HIS COTTON GIN, ELI WHITNEY WAS ACTUALLY PROUDER OF HIS OKRA BLOTTER.

Eli Whitney

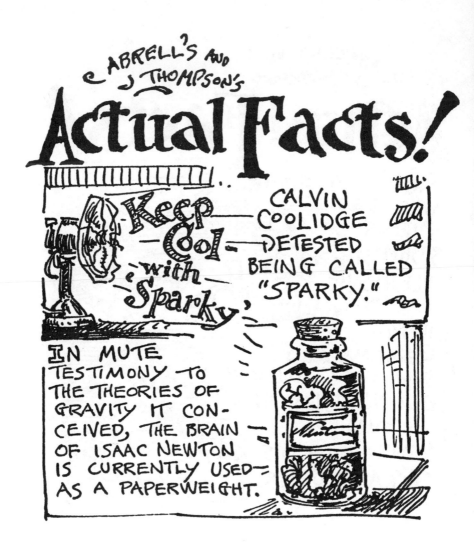

ABRELL'S AND J THOMPSON'S
Actual Facts!

Keep Cool with Sparky

CALVIN COOLIDGE DETESTED BEING CALLED "SPARKY."

IN MUTE TESTIMONY TO THE THEORIES OF GRAVITY IT CONCEIVED, THE BRAIN OF ISAAC NEWTON IS CURRENTLY USED AS A PAPERWEIGHT.

Actual Facts!

ABR L'S AND IMPSON'S

IT IS A SIGN OF THE TIMES THAT PUNCTUALITY HAS BECOME AN ANACHRONISM.

FOR 27 MONTHS DURING WW II, THE EIFFEL TOWER WAS SECRETLY USED TO TEST POTATOES.

ABRELL'S AND THOMPSON'S

Actual Facts!

PRIOR TO THE DAYS OF TOM EDISON, EARLY ELECTRIC EELS HAD TO STUN THEIR PREY WITH GAS.

IN A RARE FIT OF PIQUE TYRONE SIMMS ONCE BIT HERBERT HOOVER.

ABRELL'S AND J THOMPSON'S

Actual Facts!

CHARLIE MEDICINE HORN DISCOVERED GERMANY IN APRIL OF 1943.

IF DILUTED THINLY ENOUGH, THE JUICE OF ONE LEMON WOULD COVER THE STATE OF OREGON.

Actual Facts!

BELYING HIS
BASIC RHYTHMICAL
COMPETENCE,
FRÉDÉRIC CHOPIN
NEVER
FULLY MAS-
TERED THE
BONGOES.

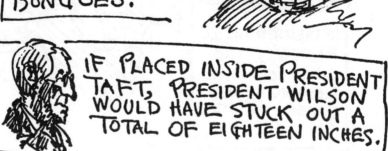

IF PLACED INSIDE PRESIDENT
TAFT, PRESIDENT WILSON
WOULD HAVE STUCK OUT A
TOTAL OF EIGHTEEN INCHES.

ABRELL'S AND J THOMPSON'S

Actual Facts!

CONGRESS AUTHORIZED FUNDS FOR THE CYCLOTRON BELIEVING IT WOULD PROMOTE PHYSICAL FITNESS.

THE MOST POPULAR EXHIBIT AT THE 1939 WORLD'S FAIR FEATURED A LUMINOUS BOWLING BALL.

Actual Facts!

ABRELL'S AND THOMPSON'S

DR. BELOIT FLEXNER WAS SENTENCED TO PRISON FOR INVENTING THE "CYMBALODEON."

COUNT OTTO VON BISMARCK HAD THE WORLD'S FINEST COLLECTION OF NAUGHTY SOUVENIR KEYCHAIN VIEWERS.

Abrell's and Thompson's Actual Facts!

FAINT MARKINGS ON THE STATUE OF LIBERTY REVEAL SHE ONCE SPORTED A WRISTWATCH.

ALTHOUGH FIRST HAILED AS "A DAZZLING ACHIEVEMENT IN GENETIC ENGINEERING," COMMERCIAL RESPONSE HAS BEEN DISAPPOINTING FOR "ANATOLE ZERT'S GIANT HOMING RATS."

ABRELL'S AND THOMPSON'S
Actual Facts!

ENVIOUS OF HIS BROTHER BEN'S SUCCESS, BOTANIST BUD FRANKLIN FOUNDED THE DISAPPOINTING <u>SATURDAY EVENING FERN</u>.

WHEREAS MOST COUNTRIES STILL HAVE A NATIONAL ANTHEM AND A NATIONAL FLAG, ONLY FOUR RETAIN A NATIONAL HAT SIZE.

ABRELL'S AND THOMPSON'S
Actual Facts!

SO-CALLED "LAP DOGS" WERE BRED TO BE EATEN.

THE GIBOON CENTIPEDE SPENDS NINE YEARS UNDERGROUND IN THE LARVAL STATE AND THEN DIES.

ABRELL'S AND THOMPSON'S
Actual Facts!

ALTHOUGH HE HAD TO ENDURE 32 PAINFUL OPERATIONS, — HAROLD "HAP" ANDERSON IS FINALLY ABLE TO PUT AN ENTIRE TELEPHONE UP HIS NOSE.

THROUGH AN OVERSIGHT, THE CONSTITUTIONAL HEIR TO THE THRONE OF AUSTRIA IS A BEAVER.

ABRELL'S AND THOMPSON'S

Actual Facts!

COSMOPOLITAN THOUGH THEY WERE, THE ANCIENT VIKINGS HAD VIRTUALLY NO FIRST-HAND KNOWLEDGE OF TOAST.

THE FIRST BICYCLE WAS NOT INVENTED— IT WAS FOUND IN A PARKING LOT NEAR LOURDES.

Abrell's and Thompson's Actual Facts!

NOW SADLY A RELIC OF SIMPLER TIMES IS THE FORGOTTEN ART OF VICTORIAN CHAIR-ARRANGING.

KING EDWARD THE SEVENTH FREQUENTLY ASKED TOTAL STRANGERS "NOT TO MEDDLE WITH HIS SPOONS."

Abrell's and Thompson's Actual Facts!

FOLLOWING THE LEAD OF ABRA-HAM LINCOLN, CALVIN COOLIDGE WROTE HIS SPEECHES ON GUM WRAPPERS.

UNITED STATES OF AMERICA

FIVE CENTS

IT WAS ONLY BY THE INTERVENTION OF FATE THAT THE "BUFFALO" NICKEL WAS NOT THE "WEASEL" NICKEL.

ABRELL'S AND THOMPSON'S
Actual Facts!

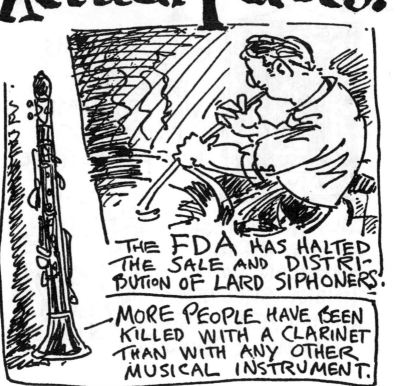

THE FDA HAS HALTED THE SALE AND DISTRIBUTION OF LARD SIPHONERS.

MORE PEOPLE HAVE BEEN KILLED WITH A CLARINET THAN WITH ANY OTHER MUSICAL INSTRUMENT.

ABRELL'S AND J THOMPSON'S
Actual Facts!

GAINSBOROUGH'S FAMOUS "BLUE BOY" WAS PURCHASED FOUR TIMES JUST FOR THE FRAME.

ONLY TWO COLLEGES ON THE NORTH AMERICAN CONTINENT STILL OFFER APPLIED ARTS COURSES IN GAS METER DECORATION.

ABRELL'S AND J THOMPSON'S

Actual Facts!

A NEW BALLET HAS BEEN SUC- CESSFULLY ADAPTED FROM A NINETEENTH CENTURY PLUMBER'S MANUAL.

A MAN CAN ACTUALLY MOVE 140 MILES PER HOUR, BUT ONLY FOR ABOUT SIX INCHES.

Abrell's and Thompson's Actual Facts!

APPARENTLY, THE ENTIRE MESO-
ZOIC ERA WAS WASTED WHILE
DINOSAURS SLOWLY EVOLVED FROM
CHICKENS, WHICH, AT THE TIME,
WEIGHED 400 TONS.

MOST OF THE NUTRITION IN
A BANANA IS CONCENTRATED
AT ONE END.

CABRELL'S AND
J THOMPSON'S

Actual Facts!

THE SHORTEST PERIOD OF TIME
IS UNMEASURABLE, AND
HAS BEEN
DUBBED
"THE MUFFY."

THE PROTOTYPE
FOR THE
ATOMIC CLOCK
BLEW UP.

ABRELL'S AND THOMPSON'S

Actual Facts!

THE MEANING OF THE WORD "MUTANT" HAS GRADUALLY CHANGED OVER THE YEARS.

•mu'tant (r

A NATURE PROGRAM ON THE LUMINOUS SLUGS OF NORWAY DELIBERATELY SHOWED THE SAME SLUG FOR ALMOST 90 MINUTES.

ABRELL'S AND THOMPSON'S
Actual Facts!

ORVILLE WRIGHT, ALTHOUGH HE WOULD CONSENT TO REPAIR THEM, REGARDED BICYCLES AS FAR TOO DANGEROUS TO RIDE.

THE WASHINGTON MONUMENT WAS DESIGNED TO BE SET IN A FIVE-HUNDRED FOOT HOLE!

Actual Facts!

ⓔ ABRELL'S AND ꞁ THOMPSON'S

TO ILLUSTRATE A POINT, FIELD MARSHAL PHALZGRAFF VON DIESELKRÄNKE FILLED HIS PARADE BOOTS WITH HAM GRAVY.

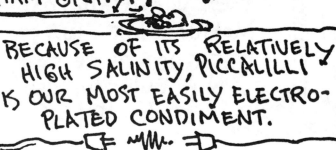

BECAUSE OF ITS RELATIVELY HIGH SALINITY, PICCALILLI IS OUR MOST EASILY ELECTRO-PLATED CONDIMENT.

Abrell's and Thompson's
Actual Facts!

A WASTE STORAGE FACILITY NEAR RUNOFF, COLORADO, CONTAINS SOME 27,000 RADIOACTIVE PANCAKE FLIPPERS.

SCIENCE HAS AT LAST FOUND A USE FOR THE FRONT PART OF LIGHTNING BUGS.

ABRELL'S AND J THOMPSON'S
Actual Facts!

BECAUSE OF A BAD EXPERIENCE DURING THE JACKSON ADMINISTRATION, PANGOLINS HAVE BEEN BANNED FROM THE WHITE HOUSE GROUNDS.

ONE OF THE MOST DIFFICULT CONCEPTS TO APPRECIATE IN THE ABSTRACT IS THAT OF SQUID LIPS.

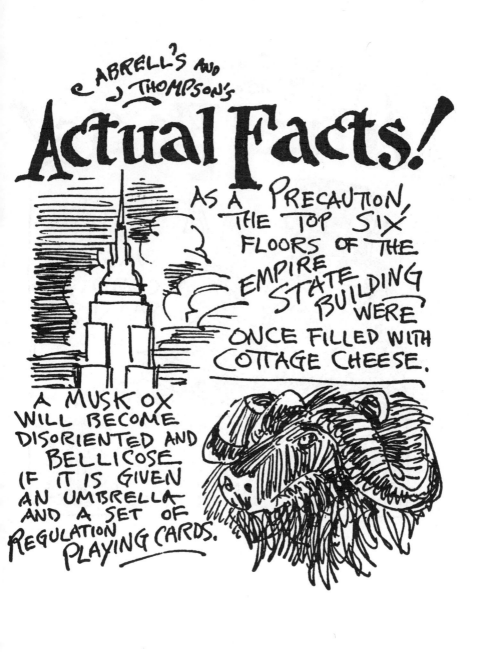

CABRELL'S AND
J THOMPSON'S

Actual Facts!

AS A PRECAUTION, THE TOP SIX FLOORS OF THE EMPIRE STATE BUILDING WERE ONCE FILLED WITH COTTAGE CHEESE.

A MUSK OX WILL BECOME DISORIENTED AND BELLICOSE IF IT IS GIVEN AN UMBRELLA AND A SET OF REGULATION PLAYING CARDS.

ABRELL'S AND THOMPSON'S
Actual Facts!

ATTILA, THE HUN, WAS AN ACCOMPLISHED PIANIST.

A CUSTODIAN OF THE BOZEMAN COUNTY COURTHOUSE SAYS A TELEPHONE IN THE LOBBY HAS BEEN RINGING CONTINUOUSLY FOR SOME 34 YEARS.

Abrell's and Thompson's Actual Facts!

STRANGELY, THE ACT OF **FORGETTING** IS THE ONLY THING WE DO THAT REQUIRES THE ENTIRE BRAIN.

IN ONE FORM OR ANOTHER, EVERYTHING WE EAT HAS BEEN EATEN BEFORE.

ABRELL'S AND THOMPSON'S

Cully Abrell's resumé incorporates a strange and lengthy array of occupations, numbering some forty—among them, carnival worker, bartender, blackjack dealer, north woods guide, and most recently, a nineteen-year university professorship.

Actual Facts!

John Thompson is something of a carpenter, mason, plumber, and electrician. He tinkers with old typewriters, repairs clocks, cameras, radios. . . . Unlike Mr. Abrell, however, Mr. Thompson has never really gotten started at anything, and now seems pretty much to have given up. He has a degree in art.

Both men live near Peck, Kansas. They have not yet been in a major tornado.

WHAT THEY ARE SAYING ABOUT THIS BOOK

"ABSOLUTELY PRICELESS. MINE COST $6.95."
— Q.E.D., MANCHESTER

"... LEARNED MORE ABOUT HATS IN FIVE MINUTES THAN I EVER THOUGHT POSSIBLE."
— H.B.M., WINCHESTER

"I HOPE THEY TAKE THAT THING ABOUT PORPOISE SEMEN OUT."
— PRINCE PHILIP

"WELL, YOU'VE CERTAINLY OPENED MY EYES ABOUT PRESIDENT TAFT."
— D.A.R. WEST CHESTER

"YOU KNOW, THAT CHAMELEON HAS PAID FOR ITSELF A THOUSAND TIMES OVER. THANKS, GUYS."
— Q-E.D., DORCHESTER

"I SAID I'D CALL YOU IN A DAY OR TWO."
— E.D., THE MAIN STREET PRESS

"I JUST CAN'T GET THAT THING ABOUT TONGUES OUT OF MY MIND. I'M GOING TO HAVE TO SHOW THIS TO MY SISTER."
— R.N., SIDNEY (NEBRASKA)